The Perfect Author

SHAY VILLERE

Copyright © 2017 Shay Villere

All rights reserved.

ISBN: 197389534X
ISBN-13: 978-1973895343

Dedicated to my teachers, who taught me how to write well, and my parents, who edited piles of my work over the years

BOOKS BY SHAY

The Line

Angelic Advice

The Angel Interviews

Bipolar Disorder Manual

Prayer to Jesus

The Intercessors Autobiography

The Hacker Angel

The Magic Man

CONTENTS

1	Doing the Impossible	3
2	The Connection	5
3	The Dynamics of Efficient Writing	7
4	Stepping Up	10
5	Firing at the Typical Villains	12
6	Stopping While People Are Still Interested	15
7	The Faster the Better	17
8	The Power	19
9	The Audience	21
10	The Danger in Danger	23
11	Cashing In	25

ACKNOWLEDGMENTS

To my fifth grade teacher Mr. Peter Masony who continually allowed me to read my twenty page spy stories out loud to the class while the rest of the students were doing two pages.

DOING THE IMPOSSIBLE

Have you ever wanted to fly, but did not feel that you ever could? Then as you are about to die, an angel walks into your room, lifts your soul out of your body, and you fly away together? Then you know you can. And it takes a great writer to provide that experience without really experiencing it. But I just did it right there.

Why do we read our favorite authors? They do the impossible. They take us to another place while you are sitting in your living room as your kids scream and your boiling water overflows. Good authors love to know they have that power. They take reality to a higher level. Have you ever wondered what life would be like without books...and books that were turned into movies? Sadness...as we would mope through one annoying task to another, not knowing there were better shores for our ship to port in.

Take a moment and ask yourself if you could ever really rewrite your life. Would you be able to change the past if given the chance? How would you describe that alternative life? What would be so different about it? You see, most folks cannot do that. But I have been living an alternative life ever since I was 16, when I almost died from bipolar disorder. I set up a portion of my mind to always run in case bipolar disorder wiped out my typical processing. How did it work out? I'm 37 now and I have an incredible wife and daughter. I expect to make several hundred thousand dollars this year. Yeah, I do think it worked out.

If you want to talk to me regarding your writing, I am more than happy to help. But you do have to find me. Why? Well, if I just gave you my info it would be so typical. And adventure is much more fun!

THE CONNECTION

How many friends do you have? Did you grow up in a small family, or a big one? Do you like to be around people?

Writing in an effective manner is often controlled by the kind of background you have. If you can create personable connections early in life, you will usually have a better chance of connecting with the reader.

I love to spend time with others. I can walk into a room of strangers and instantly make a few friends. I'm also the kind of guy who prefers solid companionship. I've been with my wife for 11 years. It is just the kind of life I enjoy. And I enjoy writing just as much.

In past years, people have tried to steer me into government work, or journalism jobs of different sorts. The reason I never took those routes is because they did not offer very much control over the creative process, and I also did not want to write so much that I would stop enjoying it. For a friendly, social, creative guy who likes to write, that would be like an early death.

Routinely folks tell me that what they truly like about my writing style is that it feels like a conversation. I did not choose to be like that. I am a personable person in real life. I have great relationships with my friends, family, and co-workers. Maybe it all flows into my writing. I don't really know. But my goal with writing is to teach. It always has been. I feel like I teach as if I was an advice columnist. You know, that friend down the street who is old and wise and loves to help. I'm not old or wise though. However I did run an advice column for a while several years ago. That was long before Yahoo Answers or eBay.

THE DYNAMICS OF EFFICIENT WRITING

Why are you burning ink? Why are you wasting so much time? What kind of direct message does that CHAPTER provide? If you have spent too much effort, it shows, and the reader knows. No one is here to waste time, so the faster the delivery the better.

Blogs do this the best. Humanity was DYING for a system of communication like this. For years and decades and centuries we have been bogged down by a system of writing that rewards publishing companies and puts readers to sleep. Now real authors are rewarded for flying to the message and not wasting readers' time. So they kick out a few minutes of work and then move on.

I wrote my first book when I was 10. It was about a British secret agent, just like James Bond. I used to revel in the fact that I had spent twenty pages on a chapter, ten times that of my classmates. I could write and write and write. My teachers loved it! But as I got older I began to fret about the useless sentences I was sometimes kicking out. My efficient brain did not want to be viewed as a creator of sludge, just to get better grades from authority figures. So as I got older, I changed.

My first website was rolled out when I was 21. It was an advice site geared toward providing fabulous information in a fast format where the whole world could benefit. What I found was that people LOVED this kind of writing! They liked helpful information in a speedy format. They were DYING to experience this kind of stuff. So on I went, creating content that shot out efficient messages, and I left the junk to other guys.

The only asset in the world that can neither be extended nor created is time. Once you have spent your time, it is gone forever and will never return. That is why I am not interested in the kind of writing that will require months of research, followed up with months of ten hour days. Writing must be efficient and it must get to your audience almost instantaneously. How do you manage this? With technology of course.

I no longer believe in traditional publishing. There are lots of ways to create audiences and move units, all without leaving your house. Right now I have seven books up for sale. I did it by writing Word docs, converting them to PDF, and uploading them to LuLu and Amazon. It was all quite easy and fun. I would not consider doing things any other way. Today's market demands speed and easy business relationships. Without that kind of supply chain speed, you simply won't have the time you need to get onto your next project.

Have you ever read the book, "How to Eat Fried Worms?" It is the only book I ever read that had a one sentence chapter. "A Tale of Two Cities" began with an forty or fifty sentence paragraph. Which do you think the reader preferred?

In today's world we just don't have time to waste. That's why you must keep things short and to the point. If you want to be long-winded, go teach somewhere. They will pay you to write boring books that no one readers, unless they are students and forced into it. I have never thought writing of that nature was worth anything. I like my business degree, but man...talk about some dry textbooks.

Let yourself take the shortest distance between two lines. Don't go on and on. Get your point across. Enjoy the writing, but frankly, if you don't keep things efficient, you will get NOWHERE. The entire world is fighting over eyeballs and earballs. If you really think you can compete with guys like me who pump out targeted content every single day in GROWING blogs...I invite you to try.

No one actually wants to read a 300 page novel that takes 100 pages just to start moving. Do you know why John Grisham books sell so well? He does not make you wait. Granted, he does some setup, but the setup is fun too. I have tried to read other fiction writers, and generally dump them in favor of Grisham, who still pumps out a novel regularly in spite of having a decades long career.

STEPPING UP

Folks, if you don't pony up in life, you will never get anywhere.

Some folks call it stepping up. Some folks call it manning up. Simpler people just describe it as trying, or putting forth effort. I prefer the easiest term, "working".

I was probably in third grade when I realized that life needed to contain some work if I ever expected to succeed at anything. I had a science test, and did not bother to study for it, figuring my inherent brilliance would get me through. Well, obviously I was wrong, as my "D" proved. My science teacher took me aside and said that I was much better than my "D" had shown, and that she expected me to work harder for the next test. Her logic seemed to make sense, especially after my parents concurred.

School really proves something. It proves to you that work pays off. And in my opinion school does a better job of that than most jobs. I have never had a job that is anywhere close to as hard as college was. The work I put out in college was so phenomenal that I was often driven to sleepless nights and bad decisions. But after getting out, and doing the corporate thing for a few years, I realized that it was never going to be that hard again, at least not because of a job.

For those of you in relationships, you know that it takes work. In fact, it probably takes more work for guys than girls. Girls get passes in relationships usually, because they hold some sort of natural power over men who are in love with them. But both partners need to work. Without putting effort out every single day, that experience just does not succeed. Writing is the same way. Without spending some sweat, you don't get anywhere.

Are you worried about having the balls to really get things done? That's everyone's problem. Do you think FDR really was not worried that we would lose WW2? Of course he was freaked out about it. But he could still sleep at night. He might ring Churchill with an idea at 2am, but it was still impressive being him. We're 70 years past all that, and most people would GLADLY swap Obama for EITHER Roosevelt.

I'm not saying that there is a special trait that good leaders have. I just think they have learned enough about life to realize that when powerful effort is fired at a good plan, then great things happen. The problem is that we have so many cooks in the kitchen at this point, getting things done can be quite hard. The G8 recently turned into the G20, or something else huge. Can you imagine how those meetings go? We doubled the size of the world's powerful countries. Do you think that makes things harder or easier? Frankly, I'm really to move my family to Fiji and live on a beach. That sounds more appealing than getting taxed into the poor house, which is what will happen otherwise.

FIRING AT THE TYPICAL VILLAINS

There is a simple truism to life: people like to see good succeed.

There are all kinds of folks in this world. Good, bad, apathetic. But stories have to include a happy ending. There is no sequel without a hero to star in it. Even in horror movies, the hero usually wins. The bible? Forget it. Satan never had a chance.

Let's look at this for a minute. Does the real world work like this? Well, kinda. But usually it is not exactly a pretty or truly pure process. Villains might go down, but not without taking millions of dead people with them. I guess you could say that good usually wins, but there is never a guarantee that the planet won't go down in a sudden inferno. So what do we do to get through the day? We pack everything into a nice little ball of faith and stick it in whatever basket we feel comfortable with.

I write a daily message to one of my Christian blogs. When I provide optimistic messages, my feedback is great. When I provide sobering, in your face messages, the feedback is not so good. So, in order to pleasure my audience into staying with me, I'm stuck. I actually believe this is a type of pandering that all broadcasters must engage in. What do you do if the audience bolts?

I have been Catholic my whole life. Every week, positive message. HOWEVER...I once saw a scathing criticism of marriage in general. I guess Catholic priests think they have a wiser view than those of us living the life. As this priest was ripping off critical comment after critical comment, you could feel the audience clenching their hindquarters. As we walked out, the facial expressions were easy to read. My dad even mentioned that the guy had guts to bring up those topics. Let's face it, pandering is safer.

Have you gotten tired of the typical hero/villain arrangement? Tough! The world wants it. The world wants it so bad that the authors of the world have been forced to feed it to the audience forever. Yes, forever! That means before the bible. What do you do if you want to write about something else? You get creative. You don't sell as many units. Then you go back to writing hero/villain stories.

I have been railing against Satan for....too long. In a lot of ways I would prefer to write about Satan Jr. or something by now. There must be an option for guys like me. However, the king of all lies who kills those in his way is hard to improve upon. Frankly, the shit streams just naturally flows toward him, as do my pithy one liners bashing him.

What I love about American politics is that when things are bad, the blame goes up the chain, not down, like in the business world. In American business we heap huge money and benefits on our top folks. When there is a significant problem, we don't really expect them to be in trouble. Usually they have golden parachutes to take care of them. So if you are a new CEO for a big company, you are in a win-win. There might be some risk, but you are not shouldering it as much as your soldiers.

Politics is completely different. Heck, we even pulled a governor out of office in California a few years ago, and stuck a movie star in his place. What was the result? A bunch of failing years for the state as a whole. We are in a much worse situation than we have been in. Heck, California might be bankrupt soon enough. Why? The accountability is not where it should be. We want to blame our leaders, and we definitely put a lot of effort toward it, but still we have no rules to make true changes to the system. Look at California to become West Nevada soon.

STOPPING WHILE PEOPLE ARE STILL INTERESTED

Your writing career is meant to go on forever. You don't write a book, and then stop. It is supposed to be a fun process that continually gives you joy, happiness, and hopefully some cash. So when you spend time writing ANYTHING...you want to leave your audience wanting more.

John Grisham is one of my favorite writers. I have not read all of his stuff, because he is so prolific and I can't keep up. However every time I finish one of his books, I have already decided to try and read the next one. That experience has been going on for about twenty years now. That kind of effect is what every writer should be shooting for.

The writing world is about creating a draw. Much of business in general is like that, but with writing it is extremely important because your next project will come along, and you'll want a reason for your readers to read it.

I was slow to pick up on the world of blogs. I really did not see their value. I thought that it would create TOO MUCH content than the world could handle. Little did I realize that blogs were soon going to be the only way to get to your audience. If you don't have a blog, you can't even get your website looked at. That being the case, if you are serious about what you're doing, it is time for you to fire up Twitter or Wordpress.

In my life I have created audiences a few times over. I'm not a New York Times bestseller, but I have been able to get my material in front of lots of eyes. Granted, my financial return has not put me in a penthouse, but I have been making progress each and every year. That is all any aspiring writer can really ask for. My bipolar manual has been read by thousands and thousands of people. My Christian prayer blog has had the same success. At this point I am working on several projects, including an angel book and an evangelism tool for other Christians to use.

Why is the bible so good? Why do people flock to it, believe in it, read it daily, study it, teach it. Why, why, why, why? I don't know. I like the bible. I actually love Jesus. But you know what? I can barely get through two or three pages of the bible. I have actually seen a modern version of the bible called The Message, but I'm not even interested enough to buy it. What I am trying to say is...why couldn't the early church create an easier read? If the book was easier to read, wouldn't there be more success? At this point, I'll probably never pick up the bible again. But you know what? The job is already done. So I suppose the bible really did leave me...still interested.

THE FASTER THE BETTER

I'm not a fan of slow writing.

I write my daily messages to my group members in less than ten minutes usually. That's roughly five seven or eight sentence paragraphs in under ten, almost every time. I don't think about them much. Many of them are very similar. But the style of my writing has proven to be somewhat hypnotic.

Dean Koontz writes for ten hours, almost daily. Stephen King MUST do something similar. But do they enjoy it? Are YOU writing to make money, or have fun? I believe that writing is only worth anything when it IS done for fun. But of course I also like getting paid for moving units.

Stop trying to connect your academic writing with your creative or communicative writing. Essays are a big joke! They have no place in the real world usually. When was the last time an essay was a best seller? I would rather write how I like and leave the footnotes and bibliographies to someone who has more time. Right now I have people to connect with, and if something gets in the way of that goal...sayonara!

THE POWER

As lots of folks are figuring out lately, there is only one power. However you choose to interpret it, there's only one. Everything came from it. Everything wants to move toward it. It gives you the power to create miracles. It gives you the power to surpass death. You really can't write effectively without some connection to it.

I was raised Catholic, but never went to parochial school. I spent a couple years in an evangelical church. I've done some research into all the big religions and philosophies. It all seems like a twist on the same thing. I'm not really sure what the arguing is about. Sometimes I think folks just like to fight in order to alleviate boredom.

Years ago I wrote a book called Angel Interviews that was intended to decipher life after this. A few folks liked it, but apparently angel talk does not sell like hotcakes. I still hold onto the thought that if I can make some other stuff move, that book will catch fire. I think it does a fabulous job of showing a different side of future life. Without the true power flowing through me, I could not have written one sentence of that book.

I only write when the power is flowing through me. In fact, unlike most writers, I only write when I'm in the mood. I do not have a certain amount of pages or hours I try to hit each weekday. I do it as I feel. That's because I have other things going on in my life, but wouldn't you prefer three quality pages every other day instead of twenty pages of garbage?

THE AUDIENCE

I think about my audience a lot. In my world, my folks are usually Christians. But obviously 3/4 of the world is NOT Christian, so obviously at some point I'll have the need to change my strategy.

What do you see when you look at your readers? My biggest problem is that I tend to dish out what I want and worry about my audience second. My blogs are membership arrangements, so if people don't like what I write, they can bail.

Do you notice how the world has been diced into demographics to such a degree that you can literally aim your message at a single type of person? All Hispanic 24 year old's. Piece of cake. It is not even a challenge for Facebook. That is their big marketing draw. Advertise with us and NAIL your target demo. That is the direction of the world now. Perfect, exact, audience targeting.

I tend to treat my audience as if they were my children. This approach serves two purposes. First, I obviously put lots of care and effort into anything my children might consume or observe. Second, I want whatever I provide to my children to hold a supreme benefit to them. I'm not going to waste my child's time. I have my child's best interest at heart.

Lots of authors seem like they are trying to impress their audience. I don't really like this approach. I like to side with the authors who are more interested in conveying personable truth. The authors who feel like your friends are the best at weaving stuff into YOUR emotions. The best thing about the television series, "Friends", is that those characters were written so well for the audience, that they felt like your actual friends.

THE DANGER IN DANGER

For about the last fifteen years, my writing has focused on improving lives and making people feel good, rather than the drearier sides of life. Obviously horror and sci-fi and all the other bizarre stuff hits a certain niche with certain people, but I tend to believe that people coming back to sugar rather than vinegar.

Take a moment to evaluate your own thoughts. Which ones make you feel good? Which thoughts are genuinely useful? Do other people enjoy what you have to say, or are you always fighting with others? The proof really has to be in the pudding. If you cannot carry on a peaceful happy life, then your writing will tend to swing toward the dour side. I enjoy dark thrillers or adventure movies, but you know what? Most folks do not want to live that way, so they will not appreciate three hundred pages of it.

My non-fiction writing is a big deal to me. I guide people toward certain sources of information in the hope that it makes things better. The funny thing is that life is probably the most scary thing there is. If we truly always spoke the truth and had nothing but honest discussions, the stark reality might be too much for most. Christian faith, and other faiths, do their best to make our situation look as good as it can, but guarantees? Nope. They were never there and they never will be. That is why they are called faiths. There is no proof included.

My relationships tend to lean toward the positive, due to the overwhelming nature of my typically exuberant personality. People usually like to hang around me. I have many friends, that I get to see pretty regularly. The reason for all of this? I'm usually spreading happiness everywhere. In writing and in life, most folks enjoy optimism.

When I was younger my writing always focused around secret agents. I thought that was the best way to live life. Fast cars and fast women. Packing a gun with the right to use it. It was the coolest....to an eleven year old boy. But as I got older what I realized is that you cannot live a life like that, and always be happy about it. Right now my writing is completely different, because I have found much better stuff to focus on...success...and the Christ.

Take it from a guy who has walked both sides of the line. Let your writing smile more than frown. Not only will you get more readers that way, but you will enjoy the process more. Plus you might find that it acts as therapy for you. Focusing on positive writing projects is a great way to enjoy your day. If I had more creativity, I would never stop writing. I just happen to enjoy it that much!

CASHING IN

What's the best subject to write about? Success, in whatever form matches the niche you are trying to hit.

For the longest time I tried to solve people's problems through an advice site. I thought I was doing a great job, but the site never hit all the spots I wanted it to. People never seemed to ask the right questions so I could lead them toward the really interesting answers. Soon enough I just realized that I should do the directing and wipe out the asking completely. So I started writing about the best way to live life.

One of the things I like to point out to people is how obsolete most jobs are. So I tend to focus on that quite a bit. The nice thing is that it is fun to talk about how the world is now, and all the opportunity out there. Most people do not know how to truly make a living online, but I've been doing it for a while now. Staying on topics like that is a great way to keep people interested, because most folks do not want to be stuck in a bad job. They are aggressively looking for options, so when I show up with some answers it is like a miracle has arrived.

There are lots of books that can give you all the information you need to write about success. Obviously there is the law of attraction, and all the experts that teach that. Also, there are books that focus on how to make your workdays condense into a few hours, rather than 8 to 16, which is what some folks work. That kind of information is like spun gold to the parts of the world that feel like they are slaves...because in a way they are.

Let's face it, everyone wants success, in some form or another. If you focus on that subject, regardless of the channel or niche you are hitting, you will always get some readers. There is simply too much new information on success building, and way too many sources of information to draw from that you can then pass along to your readers.

Small tip: For sources of information I suggest audiobooks. They are cheap, easy, and you can listen to them over and over again. Then once you have digested the information, you can start putting your own interpretation on it, and bam, you have some really great material for your readers. Remember that lots of people in the world have no idea how to produce really great success, so they tend to gobble up material like that.

THE PERFECT AUTHOR

SHAY VILLERE